YOU MUST REMEMBER THIS

1960

MILESTONES, MEMORIES,
TRIVIA AND FACTS, NEWS EVENTS,
PROMINENT PERSONALITIES &
SPORTS HIGHLIGHTS OF THE YEAR

TO : my baby brother

FROM : becky

MESSAGE : Happy Birthday!

selected and researched
by
mary a. pradt

WARNER ⓦ TREASURES ™

PUBLISHED BY WARNER BOOKS

A TIME WARNER COMPANY

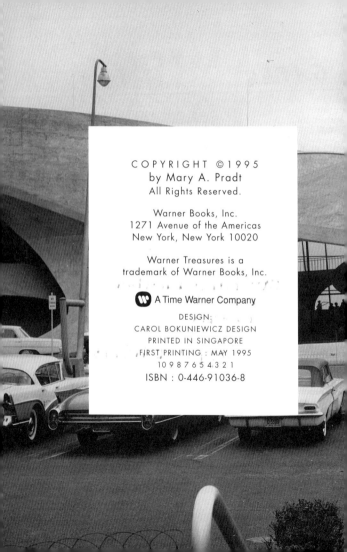

Warner Books, Inc.
1271 Avenue of the Americas
New York, New York 10020

Warner Treasures is a
trademark of Warner Books, Inc.

Ⓦ A Time Warner Company

DESIGN:
CAROL BOKUNIEWICZ DESIGN
PRINTED IN SINGAPORE
FIRST PRINTING : MAY 1995
10 9 8 7 6 5 4 3 2 1
ISBN : 0-446-91036-8

the u.s. presidential campaign

proved full of superlatives and history-making details. The Democratic ticket of John F. Kennedy and Lyndon Baines Johnson won over the Republicans' Richard M. Nixon and Henry Cabot Lodge, but by a razor-thin popular vote margin—just over 100,000 voters. It was the first presidential election in which TV played a key role; the candidates' debates were televised for the first time. On seeing a videotape of one of his TV appearances, Kennedy admitted, "We wouldn't have had a prayer without that gadget." Kennedy promised his administration would emulate FDR's "100 Days" with groundbreaking legislation and programs—everything from a "peace corps" of draft-age people to progress in civil rights.

The year 1960 was breathtaking; the pace was space-age.

FLASH!

In May, the Soviets shot down the American U-2 spy plane, which they caught making an aerial reconnaissance flight over a military installation on May Day. The pilot, Lieutenant Francis Gary Powers, was taken prisoner and given a show trial in Moscow, sentenced in August to 10 years in prison, but ultimately swapped for a Soviet spy in 1962.

newsreel

ON DECEMBER 16, TWO AIRLINERS FLYING IN SLEET AND FOG COLLIDED OVER NEW YORK CITY IN THE WORST AVIATION DISASTER IN U.S. HISTORY.

In February 1960, in Greensboro, NC, four Black students staged the first "sit-in," refusing to leave a Woolworth's counter where they were denied service. Within a year and a half, more than 70,000 students and others, Black and white, participated in sit-in demonstrations at various locations where racial discrimination was entrenched.

3

headlines

nikita khrushchev

threw a dramatic hissy fit at the UN General Assembly in October. He heaped abuse on a Philippine diplomat he considered a Western "lackey," then removed his right shoe, brandished it at the diplomat, and pounded it on the table. He had also banged with his fist while Secretary General Dag Hammarskjold spoke during this UN session.

ALL MAPS OF AFRICA HAD TO BE REDRAWN AS ONE AFTER ANOTHER, FORMER EUROPEAN COLONIES BECAME INDEPENDENT. THE YEAR 1960 WITNESSED THE BIRTH OF DAHOMEY, NIGER, UPPER VOLTA (LATER BURKINA FASO), IVORY COAST, CHAD, GABON, SOMALIA, AND MADAGASCAR. THE NEW REPUBLIC IN FORMER BELGIAN CONGO WAS THE RESULT OF A PARTICULARLY BLOODY BIRTH. THE KATANGA PROVINCE, THE CONGO'S MINERAL-RICH AREA, PULLED OUT OF THE REPUBLIC, AND A CIVIL WAR BEGAN. MANY EUROPEANS WERE KILLED OR FLED FOR THEIR LIVES.

THE CITY OF AGADIR, MOROCCO, WAS DESTROYED IN MARCH BY EARTHQUAKES, TIDAL WAVES, AND FIRE.

Communist party and government officials in China announced an intensive campaign to spread Maoist doctrine to the masses, through socialist reeducation and propaganda techniques.

yabba dabba doo.

"The Flintstones," the first TV cartoon with adult appeal and the first developed expressly for TV, premiered on ABC, where it aired Fridays at 8:30. It introduced viewers to a normal, split-level suburban family who just happened to live in the Stone Age. We met Fred and Wilma Flintstone, their neighbors the Rubbles, and other denizens of Bedrock.

Camelot would not arrive in the White House until Inauguration Day 1961, but *Camelot,* the memorable musical, arrived on Broadway after a rocky trip. It featured Richard Burton as a boyish King Arthur, Julie Andrews as his Queen Guinevere, and Robert Goulet as Sir Lancelot.

Elvis was discharged from the Army, appeared on the "Ed Sullivan Show," and met Frank Sinatra. Doobie-doobie-doo.

'60

cultural milestones

There were many signs of an emerging youth-dominated culture. The Newport Folk Festival in June ended with a "hootenanny," in which amateurs were allowed up onstage. The festival featured tributes to the ailing Woody Guthrie, with performances by Flatt & Scruggs, Pete Seeger, and a teenaged Joan Baez.

Bye, Bye, Birdie, with Dick Van Dyke, Chita Rivera, and a flock of teenagers, opened on Broadway in April. Birdie was an Elvis-like pop singer with the talent of driving teenagers wild.

game shows such as "The Price Is Right" and "What's My Line?" were impervious to "fixing" and were much cheaper productions than the big quiz shows had been.

television

top-rated shows of the fall 1960 season :

1. "Gunsmoke" (CBS)

2. "Wagon Train" (NBC)

3. "Have Gun, Will Travel" (CBS)

4. "The Andy Griffith Show" (CBS)

5. "The Real McCoys" (ABC)

6. "Rawhide" (CBS)

7. "Candid Camera" (CBS)

8. "The Untouchables" (ABC)

9. "The Price Is Right" (NBC)

10. "The Jack Benny Show" (CBS)

11. "Dennis the Menace" (CBS)

12. "The Danny Thomas Show" (CBS)

13. "My Three Sons" (ABC)

14. "77 Sunset Strip" (ABC)

15. "The Ed Sullivan Show" (CBS)

british princess margaret rose,

sister of Queen Elizabeth II, was married May 6 at Westminster Abbey to a commoner, Anthony Armstrong-Jones.

celeb wedding of the year

milestones

'60

THERE WERE RUMORS ABOUT **YVES MONTAND** AND **MONROE** WHILE THEY MADE *LET'S MAKE LOVE*, BUT MARILYN WAS STILL WED TO **ARTHUR MILLER** AND YVES TO **SIMONE SIGNORET**, SO YVES WAS GENTLEMANLY AND GALLANT AND MARILYN LADYLIKE AND DEMURE IN DENYING ANY LIAISON.

SPLITSVILLE

Aristotle Onassis, 54, the Greek shipping tycoon, was divorced from Athina "Tina" Livanos Onassis, 29. Soprano Maria Callas, 36, who was separated from her Italian husband, was reportedly the "other woman" in the affair. Callas and Onassis were seen on the yacht *Christina* and even went ashore in Monaco to dine with Prince Rainier and Princess Grace.

DEATHS

Albert Camus,
French novelist, essayist, and playwright, was killed in an auto accident at 46, in France.

Clark Gable
died in Hollywood at 59 in November. He had aggravated his heart ailment by insisting on doing his own stunts on his last film, *The Misfits*.

Oscar Hammerstein II,
America's premier lyricist, 65, died August 23, remembered for "Old Man River" and "The Last Time I Saw Paris," for the words of *South Pacific* and *The Sound of Music*.

Emily Post,
etiquette authority, died at 86 on September 25.

John D. Rockefeller, Jr.,
millionaire and philanthropist, died at 86 in May 1960.

births

PRINCE ANDREW ALBERT CHRISTIAN EDWARD, the Duke of York, Her Majesty Queen Elizabeth's second son, was born February 19. Later husband of (now estranged) Sarah Ferguson and father of Princesses Beatrice and Eugenie.

JOHN F. KENNEDY, JR., America's equivalent of the crown prince, was born November 25.

FRANK VIOLA, baseball player, was born April 19.

IVAN LENDL, tennis star, was born March 7.

STEVE CAUTHEN, jockey, was born May 1.

GREG LOUGANIS, diver, was born January 29.

JOHN ELWAY, football player, was born June 28.

JOAN JETT, singer, was born September 22.

BRANFORD MARSALIS, musician, was born August 26.

BONO, lead vocalist for U2 (named after the U.S. spy plane shot down May Day 1960), was born Paul Hewson in Dublin on May 10, 1960.

VALERIE BERTINELLI, actress, was born April 23.

CAROL ALT, model, was born December 1.

KIM ALEXIS, model, was born July 15.

Elvis, Elvis, Elvis

"Stuck on You" "It's Now or Never"

hit music

ELLA FITZGERALD AND **RAY CHARLES** WERE AWARDED LP GRAMMY AWARDS.

comedy albums

became popular. Shelley Berman was considered incredibly hip. Bob Newhart's "Button-Down Mind" album won a Best Album Grammy award. Mort Sahl was on vinyl and on the cover of *Time*.

teen angel Mark Dinning. What makes a teen angel? A tragic, bloody car crash, of course. "Teen angel, can you hear me? Teen angel, are you near me? Are you somewhere up above, and are you still my love?"

running bear (the Indian brave who loved little White Dove), performed by Johnny Preston.

i'm sorry, Brenda Lee wailed—"so sorry. Please accept my ap-ol-o-gy. . . 'cuz I was wrong and I was too blind to see."

he'll have to go—Jim Reeves explained what the other man would have to do; this spawned several rejoinder songs with the same banal melody—"She'll Have to Go," "He'll Have to Stay," etc. etc.

cathy's clown—the Everly Brothers harmonized.

theme from *a summer place* by Percy Faith and his orchestra, was romantic and danceable.

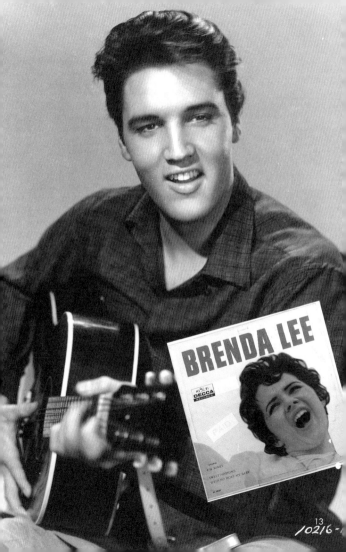

bestselling

fiction

1. **advise and consent**
   allen drury

2. **hawaii**
   james a. michener

3. **the leopard**
   giuseppe di lampedusa

4. **the chapman report**
   irving wallace

5. **ourselves to know**
   john o'hara

6. **the constant image**
   marcia davenport

7. **the lovely ambition**
   mary ellen chase

8. **the listener**
   taylor caldwell

9. **trustee from the toolroom**
   nevil shute

10. **sermons and soda-water**
    john o'hara

A good year for JOHN O'HARA, the first novelist in 25 years (after James Hilton in 1935) to have two books on an annual bestseller list.

books

1. **folk medicine**
   d. c. jarvis

2. **better homes and gardens first aid for your family**

3. **the general foods kitchens cookbook**

4. **may this house be safe from tigers**
   alexander king

5. **better homes and gardens dessert book**

6. **better homes and gardens decorating ideas**

7. **the rise and fall of the third reich**
   william l. shirer*

8. **the conscience of a conservative**
   barry goldwater

9. **i kid you not**
   jack paar

10. **between you, me and the gatepost**
    pat boone

NONFICTION BESTSELLERS WERE BEGINNING TO OUTSELL THE FICTION LISTMAKERS, REVERSING THE PREVIOUS PATTERN OF DECADES.

*SHIRER'S HISTORICAL TOME WAS AN IMPRESSIVE SUCCESS. IN TWO MONTHS, IT SOLD 111,871 COPIES, AT $10 APIECE. IN ADDITION, BOOK-OF-THE-MONTH CLUB PRINTED 270,000 MORE COPIES.

Bobby Richardson's record-breaking series for the Yankees—he drove in 12 runs. After the Yankees' success, Casey Stengel, 70, the manager, was canned. Ted Williams retired. In his final turn at bat September 28, the Boston Red Sox star hit a 420' home run  against the Baltimore Orioles. He was going to quit after a three-game series against the Yankees, but instead went out with a flourish after hitting his 521st career homer. Only Babe Ruth and Jimmy Foxx exceeded his record.

THE NFL EXPAND-ED TO 13 TEAMS WITH THE DALLAS COWBOYS (WHO HAD NO WINS IN FIRST SEASON) AND, EARLY IN 1961, MINNEAPOLIS-ST. PAUL.

G O L F

Arnold Palmer was undisputed king of the links. He won the Masters in April and the U.S. Open in June, both with heart-stopping finishes. At the Open, he shot a 6-under-par 65 to win, after going into the final round trailing by seven strokes. Palmer collected more than $80,000 in tournament play, setting a record for winnings in the sport.

floyd patterson

regained the championship and avenged his humiliating defeat by Ingemar Johansson; this was the first time a heavyweight champ had regained the title.

Wilt "the Stilt" Chamberlain broke 8 NBA records.

sports

HORSE RACING KELSO, WHO DID NOT RACE IN ANY OF THE TRIPLE CROWN TOURNEYS, WON 3-YEAR-OLD AND AMERICAN HONORS.

O L Y M P I C S

EASIER AIR TRAVEL MADE OLYMPIC ATTENDANCE SWELL. THE SUMMER OLYMPICS WERE HELD IN ROME, THE WINTER OLYMPICS IN SQUAW VALLEY, CA. WILMA RUDOLPH, "THE BLACK GAZELLE," TOOK THREE GOLD MEDALS FOR AMERICA. RAFER JOHNSON, A BLACK ATHLETE FROM CALIFORNIA, WON THE DECATHLON. CHRIS VON SALTZA LED THE AMERICANS IN WOMEN'S SWIMMING. AN ETHIOPIAN RUNNER, ABEBE BIKILA, RAN AND WON THE MARATHON BAREFOOTED. CASSIUS CLAY, 18, TOOK OLYMPIC GOLD IN BOXING, DEFEATING POLISH CONTENDER ZIGGY PIETRZYKOWSKI.

17

Billy Wilder's ***The Apartment*** dominated the Academy Awards, named as Best Picture over *The Alamo*, *Elmer Gantry*, *Sons and Lovers*, and *The Sundowners*. Wilder took the directing Oscar over Jack Cardiff (for *Sons and Lovers*), Jules Dassin (for *Never On Sunday*), Fred Zinnemann (for *Sundowners*), and Alfred Hitchcock (nominated for *Psycho*). **Burt Lancaster,** as Elmer Gantry, got Best Actor honors, over Trevor Howard, Jack Lemmon, Laurence Olivier, and Spencer Tracy. **Elizabeth Taylor** was named Best Actress for her role in ***Butterfield 8.*** The other nominees were Greer Garson, Deborah Kerr, Shirley MacLaine, and Melina Mercouri. **Peter Ustinov** got Supporting Actor Oscar for his role in ***Spartacus,*** while **Shirley Jones** won as Best Supporting Actress, for ***Elmer Gantry.*** The Swedish import ***The Virgin Spring*** won Foreign Language Oscar.

'60

THERE WAS A GROWING VOGUE FOR FOREIGN FILMS—THE FRENCH **HIROSHIMA MON AMOUR,** THE GREEK **NEVER ON SUNDAY,** AND THE MUCH-HONORED ITALIAN FILM **LA DOLCE VITA.**

movies

top grossing movies of 1960

1. Ben-Hur
2. Psycho
3. Operation Petticoat
4. Suddenly, Last Summer
5. On the Beach
6. Solomon and Sheba
7. The Apartment
8. From the Terrace
9. Please Don't Eat the Daisies
10. Oceans Eleven

Somebody did a big U-turn; suddenly, it seemed, the emphasis was on economy and simplicity, not horsepower and glamor. Six new compact cars were available, including Ford's second compact, the Comet (first was the Falcon). The new Dodge Dart, though a standard-sized car, was more compact and boxy-looking. Even

cars

the luxury cars, like the Caddy, got shorter and had fewer frilly details. American Motors' Rambler station wagon, with five doors and three seats, sold well in the 'burbs; a swing-out back door replaced the tailgate.

Led by Ford and matched by the other majors, American car companies had enough confidence in the quality of their products to offer, for the first time, 12-month or 12,000-mile warranties for new cars.

The casual, "leggier" youthful look was beginning to influence fashion. Hemlines, mind you, were still measured *from the floor*, and 19″ was very daring. Skirts were still mostly bouffant, likewise hair and hats, unless hair was in a short bob with points on each cheek. Loosely wrapped tulle

the leopard coat was perhaps the ultimate status symbol

fashion

helmet hats for evening were at every hat counter. Dresses and ensembles had a looser, blousier silhouette; the overall look—sculptural and architectural, with a tall, slender, narrow oval effect. Vaguely "spacey." Opulent rich colors were popular, as were luxurious and obviously expensive fabrics, styled, perhaps in short, ruffly party dresses, maybe with beaded or sequined matching jackets.

menswear

was slowly starting to reflect the import influence, with some acceptance of British and Italian stylings. For most men, it would take the whole decade for the guy in the gray flannel cocoon to emerge as a Monarch butterfly—or peacock.

final factoid

an electronic telephone exchange

developed by Bell Labs could handle calls 1,000 times faster than existing technology, with early versions of speed dial and call-forwarding functions, and the Post Office tested its first facsimile mail system, in which letters would be scanned electronically and transmitted to a faraway location in seconds.

archive photos: inside front cover, pages 1, 5, 11, 15, 21, 23, 25, inside back cover.

associated press: pages 2, 4, 10, 16.

photofest: pages 6, 8, 9, 13, 18, 19.

original photography:
beth phillips: page 13.

album cover:
courtesy of bob george/
the archive of contemporary music: page 13

photo research:
alice albert

coordination:
rustyn birch

design:
carol bokuniewicz design
mutsumi hyuga

'60